# KEY STAGE 2

# Energy, forces and communication

Jacqueline Dineen

Published by the Press Syndicate of the
University of Cambridge
The Pitt Building, Trumpington Street,
Cambridge CB2 1RP
40 West 20th Street, New York,
NY 10011-4211, USA
10 Stamford Road, Oakleigh,
Victoria 3166, Australia

© Cambridge University Press 1992

First published 1992

Designed by Steve Knowlden and Pardoe Blacker Publishing Ltd, Shawlands Court, Newchapel Road, Lingfield, Surrey RH7 6BL
Illustrated by Annabelle Brend, Neil Bulpitt, Chris Forsey, Jenny Mumford and Paul Williams

Printed in Great Britain by Scotprint Ltd, Musselburgh, Scotland.

A catalogue record for this book is available from the British Library

ISBN 0 521 39754 5

## Photographic credits

*t=top  b=bottom  c=centre  l=left  r=right*

Cover: Science Photo Library

4*b* Trevor Hill; 4/5*t* R. Wells/ZEFA; 6*t* British Coal Corporation; 7*t* Mail Newspapers/Solo; 10/11*t* J. Carnemolla/NHPA; 11*b* Mail Newspapers/Solo; 13*c* Adrian Meredith; 14*b* Landscape Only; 15*c*, 18*t*, 19*c* Trevor Hill; 21*b* Ivan Polunin/NHPA; 23*t* ZEFA; 26 Shell Photographic Service; 29*b* ZEFA; 33*t* Trevor Hill; 34*b* Jon Williams; 34/35*c* The Mansell Collection; 36*t* National Power Picture Unit; 37*t* Stephen Krasemann/NHPA; 39*r* National Grid; 41*r* Trevor Hill; 43*t* J & M. Bain/NHPA; 44*t*, 44*b* Jon Williams; 47*c* P. Degginger/ZEFA; 49*t* Ralph & Daphne Keller/NHPA; 49*b* Anthony Bannister/NHPA; 51*l* Trevor Hill; 51*r* P. Saloutos/ZEFA; 53*l*, 53*r* Trevor Hill; 54*t* The Mansell Collection; 55*b* British Telecommunications plc; 57*t* Adrian Meredith; 57*b* The Mansell Collection; 59*l* BBC; 60*t* Ford/Dagenham; 60*bl*, 60*br* Trevor Hill.

---

**NOTICE TO TEACHERS**
The contents of this book are in the copyright of Cambridge University Press. Unauthorised copying of any of the pages is not only illegal but also goes against the interests of the author.
For authorised copying please check that your school has a licence (through the Local Education Authority) from the Copyright Licensing Agency which enables you to copy small parts of the text in limited numbers.

# Contents

| | | | |
|---|---|---|---|
| Introduction | 4 | Carrying electricity and gas | 38 |
| Using energy | 6 | Heat | 40 |
| Force | 8 | Light | 42 |
| Going faster | 10 | Sound | 48 |
| Slowing down | 12 | Recording sound | 50 |
| Moving loads | 14 | Sending messages by wire | 52 |
| Using wind energy | 20 | The telephone | 54 |
| Using water energy | 22 | Sending messages without wires | 56 |
| How fuels formed | 24 | Television | 58 |
| Using fuels | 30 | Computers | 60 |
| Electricity | 32 | Key words | 62 |
| Magnets and electricity | 34 | Index | 64 |
| Generating electricity | 36 | | |

# Introduction

There would be no life on Earth without **energy**. You need energy all the time. Even when you are asleep, you breathe and your heart beats. This could not happen without energy.

Animals need energy to live and move. Plants need energy to live and grow. Machines need energy to work.

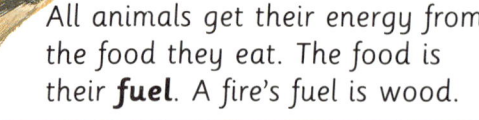

Find out more about how your body works in the *New Horizons* book, *Look you! Look me!*

All animals get their energy from the food they eat. The food is their **fuel**. A fire's fuel is wood.

## Making work easier

People have found ways to **transfer** energy efficiently. They have invented machines which make work easier. They have learned how to transfer energy from fuels into electricity. Energy can be transferred from electricity into light and heat.

What other tasks can energy do?

**Did you know...?**
The word 'energy' comes from the Greek word 'ergon' which means 'work'.

## Energy transfer

Energy from the Sun keeps everything on the Earth alive. When plants grow, they take in **carbon dioxide** gas from the air and water from the soil. They transfer energy from the Sun into the food they make.

A flash of lightning lights up the sky during a thunderstorm. Energy from the **electric charge** is transferred into the air as light, heat and sound.

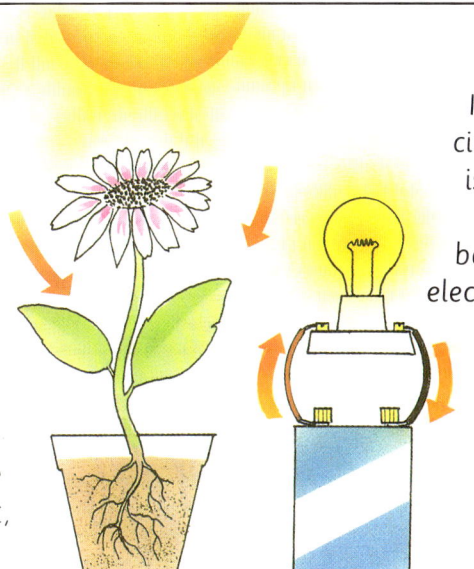

In an electric circuit, energy is transferred from the battery to the electricity which flows to a bulb. In the bulb, this energy is transferred into light and heat.

More about: electricity pp30-39  light pp42-47  sound pp48-51, 54-57

# Using energy

Energy can be stored. It can be released to do useful work. It can make things move, heat things, make noises or make light.

A tree gets its energy from the Sun.

Coal was formed from trees which died millions of years ago. The stored energy is still there, waiting to be released when you burn the coal.

Energy is stored in the wood, leaves and fruit.

When the tree dies, the energy is not destroyed.

If the wood is burned, the energy is transferred and spreads out to heat the air. Spread-out energy is less useful for doing work.

Your body uses the stored energy in your food. The energy is stored in your **muscles** and enables you to do work like running or breathing!

You can transfer energy to something else. When you throw a ball, you use energy. As you let go, the work your arm has done makes the ball fly forward. The ball now has moving energy.

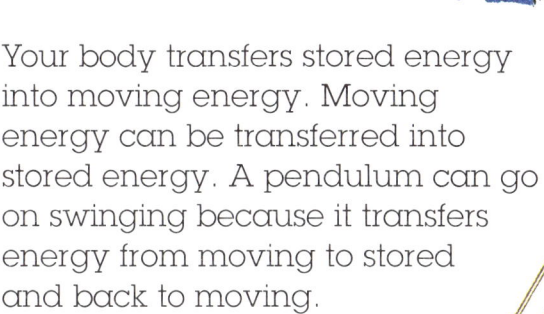

Your body transfers stored energy into moving energy. Moving energy can be transferred into stored energy. A pendulum can go on swinging because it transfers energy from moving to stored and back to moving.

When you push the pendulum, your energy is passed to it as stored energy. It uses energy to swing.

As it swings downwards, it moves faster. The moving energy is greatest here, and the stored energy least.

As it swings upwards, it slows to a stop before it starts moving back again. The moving energy is transferred back to stored energy.

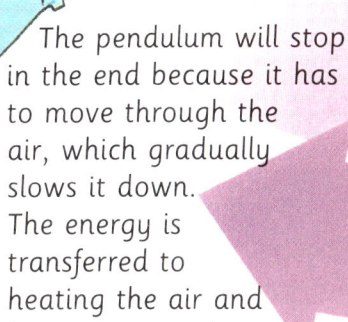

The pendulum will stop in the end because it has to move through the air, which gradually slows it down. The energy is transferred to heating the air and becomes spread out.

When the pendulum swings back the other way, the stored energy is transferred back to moving energy.

More about: acceleration pp10-11  coal pp25-27  friction pp12-15

# Force

Objects need a push or a pull to make them move, change direction, change speed or stop. This push or pull is called force. Force can also make objects change shape.

## How forces act

When you mould plasticene, you push and pull it to get the shape you want.

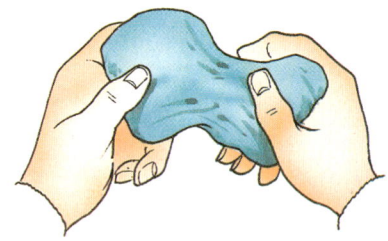

When you start to walk or run, you push your body forward. You use the force produced by your muscles.

When you fly a kite, the force upwards is stronger than gravity.

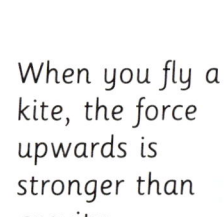

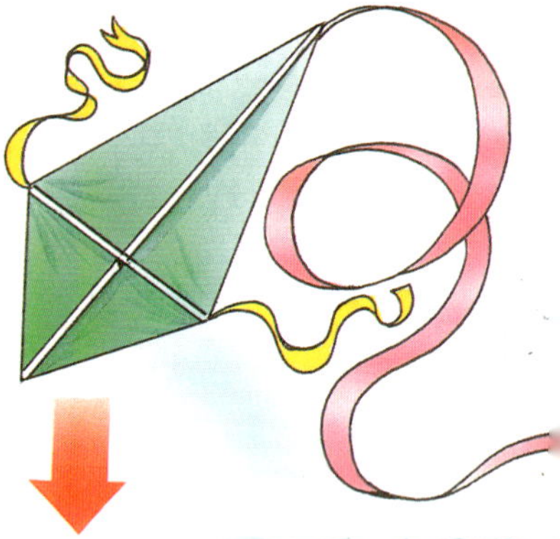

If the wind drops, gravity pulls the kite back to the ground. The force of gravity has made it fall.

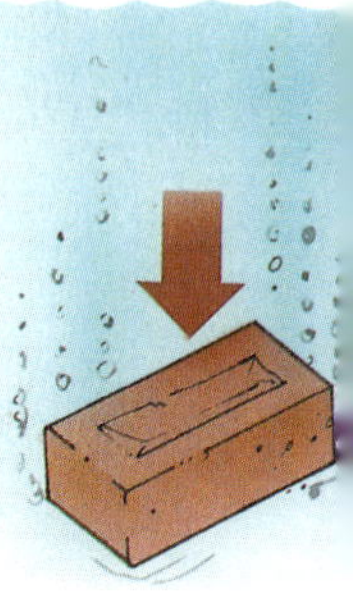

A heavy brick sinks because the pull of gravity is greater than the upward push of the water.

### Weight on the Moon

The Moon is smaller than the Earth. Its force of gravity is only one-sixth as strong. So an astronaut weighs only one-sixth of what he or she weighs on Earth. Weight is measured in newtons (N). A newton is about the weight of a large apple.

A force keeps you on the ground. This is the force of **gravity**. It is a force between you and the Earth.

If you drop an object . . .

. . . it falls to the ground.

Gravity pulls the object to the ground (and the ground to the object!).

Weight is the force of gravity or the amount of pull on an object. A big rock is heavy because of the pull of gravity.

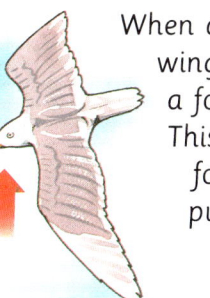

When a bird flaps its wings, it produces a force called lift. This balances the force of gravity pulling it down.

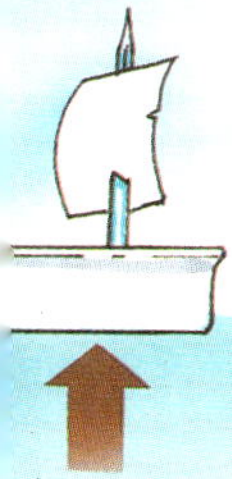

When an object floats, the weight of the object is balanced by an upwards force known as upthrust. The more liquid an object **displaces** or pushes aside, the greater the upthrust.

What happens if you put a lump of plasticene into water? What happens if you shape it into a boat? What does this tell you? Which forces are acting on the plasticene?

Force makes water flow. Why does a river flow downhill?

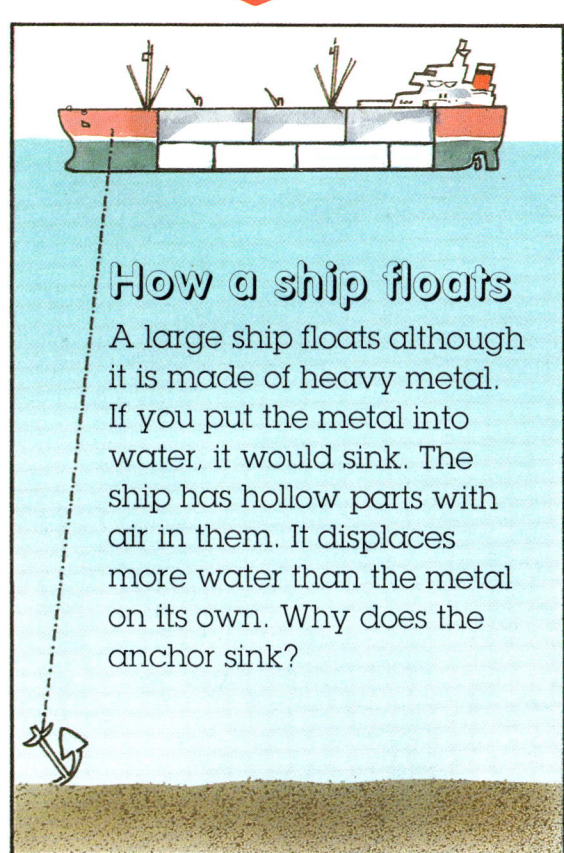

## How a ship floats

A large ship floats although it is made of heavy metal. If you put the metal into water, it would sink. The ship has hollow parts with air in them. It displaces more water than the metal on its own. Why does the anchor sink?

More about: forces pp10-23  water energy pp22-23

# Going faster

The measure of how fast something is moving is called its **speed**. An object's speed depends on its size and the size of the force used to get it going. The greater the force, the greater the speed. Speeding up is called **acceleration**.

A car with a powerful engine will accelerate more quickly than the same size car with a less powerful engine. The more powerful engine exerts more force, and so it accelerates more quickly.

## Gravity and speed

If you are pedalling your bicycle on a flat road and there is no wind against you, the harder you pedal, the faster you go.

When you go downhill, you do not need to pedal. Gravity is moving you.

When an object 'falls' it gets faster.

## Wind force

A strong wind behind you blows you along. You can walk at the same speed *against* a strong wind, but it is hard work. The force of the wind can be so strong that it causes damage. Buildings have to be carefully designed so that they do not blow down.

## Gravity tests

What happens if you drop a heavy object and a light object together from the same height? Will the heavy object hit the ground first?

Drop two identical marbles from different heights into soft mud or sand. Which makes the biggest dent? Why?

Look back to the pendulum on page 7. Name the force which starts it swinging from one side. Which force makes it move faster as it swings?

Find out about buildings in *What is it made of?*, and wind force in *Land, water and air*, both New Horizons books.

Boats with sails use the force of the wind to move along. The stronger the wind, the faster the boat goes. Does the size of the sail make a difference?

## Did you know...?

- The cheetah is the fastest **mammal** on Earth. It uses the force of its strong muscles to accelerate to 110 km/h as it chases its **prey**.
- Kangaroos have long, strong back legs. They leap about 8 m at a time at a speed of 65 km/h.

More about: gravity pp8-9  wind energy pp20-21

# Slowing down

A wheel moves because a force acts on it. The wheel will not roll on for ever, though.

You have to pedal your bike to keep it going.

Moving through the air on your bike causes friction which slows you down.

The wheels of your bike begin to slow down because they rub against the road.

When things move, they rub against other surfaces. This causes a force called friction. **Friction** makes things slow down and stop.

## Friction and machines

Machines have moving parts which rub together. This friction slows the machine down and makes the parts wear. Machines are oiled to make the parts slide together more easily.

A rough surface causes more friction than a smooth surface. You can slide a long way on ice because there is hardly any friction. It is not easy to walk or run on ice.

If there was no friction, everything would be sliding about.

The brakes on your bike use friction.

The pads rub against the wheels and stop the bike. A car's brakes work in a similar way.

If something is moving fast, a larger force is needed to stop it than if it is moving slowly. Your bike will not stop as soon as you touch the brakes. You have to squeeze the levers hard until the bike stops. A car takes longer to stop because it is travelling much faster. Check that there are no cars coming when you cross the road, or ride your bike on to it.

If you hammer a nail into wood, friction between the wood and the nail holds the nail in place.

## Streamlining for speed

While you walk you have to push through the air, causing friction. Boats have to push through the water. Friction from the water and air slows them down. Aeroplanes, fast cars and racing boats are shaped so that the air flows round them more easily, reducing friction. This is called 'streamlining'.

Loose clothes billow out around you like a sail. The wind blows against them and slows you down.

Racing cyclists wear tight clothes to be streamlined.

More about: going faster pp10-11  oil pp25, 28-31  wind force pp20-21

# Moving loads

Early humans had only the force of their muscles to lift or carry heavy **loads**. Over thousands of years, they invented machines to help them.

## Wheels

Before the wheel was invented, people carried loads on their backs . . .

### Did you know...?
Carts with wheels were used in the Middle East more than 5000 years ago.

. . . or pulled a load along on a branch.

Then, they built simple sledges, but pulling a sledge was hard work. The whole length of the sledge rubbed against the ground, creating friction which slowed the sledge down.

They put logs of wood under their sledges to act as rollers.

The logs were chopped into pieces and put on fixed **axles**. They were the first wheels.

## Lifting in ancient times

People learned to lift giant stones thousands of years ago. Stonehenge stands on Salisbury Plain, in England. It might be an ancient temple, built nearly 5000 years ago.

14

# Using friction

Wheels travel across hard ground more easily. As the wheel can move and only a small part of it touches the ground, friction is reduced.

A wheel slows down if it sinks into soft mud or sand. Energy is used to change the shape of the mud rather than to move the vehicle.

Wheels skid on snow and ice, but sledges are ideal.

## Wheels and pulleys

Pulleys can be used to change the direction of a force. It is much easier to lift a weight using a combination of pulleys.

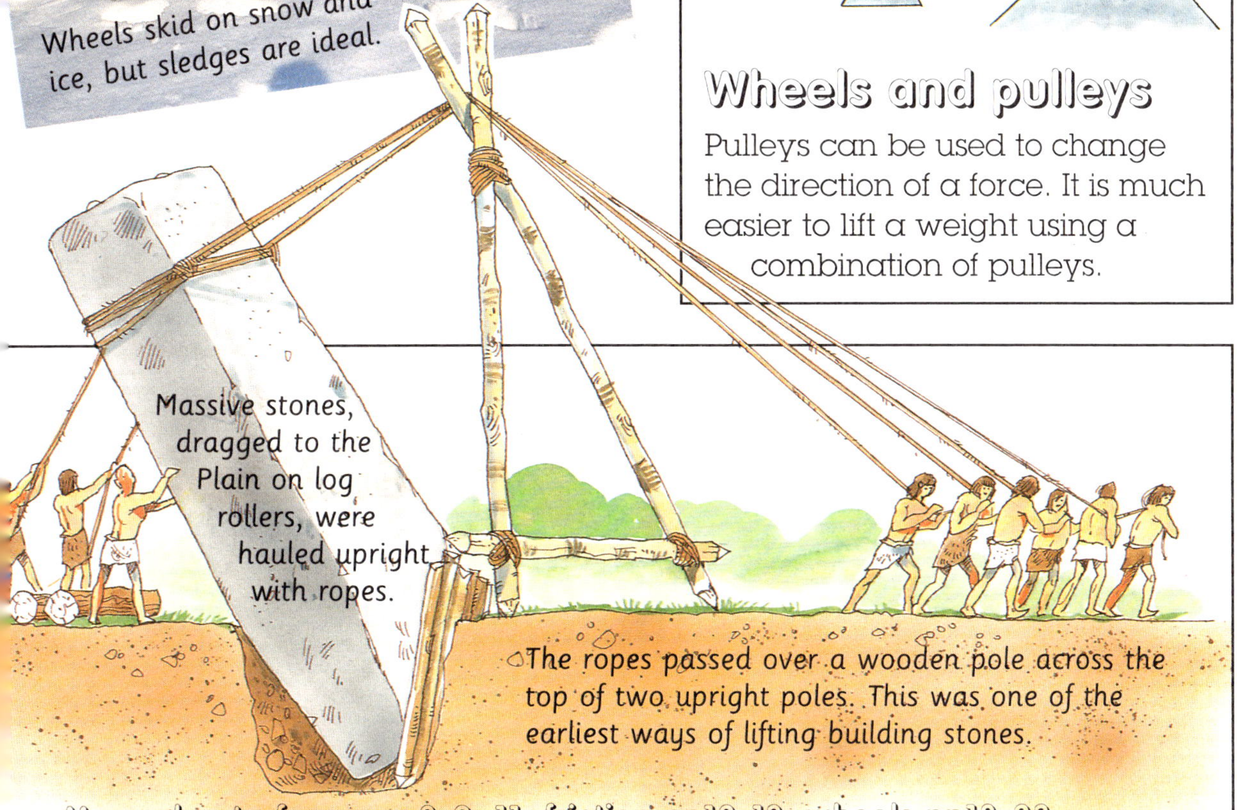

Massive stones, dragged to the Plain on log rollers, were hauled upright with ropes.

The ropes passed over a wooden pole across the top of two upright poles. This was one of the earliest ways of lifting building stones.

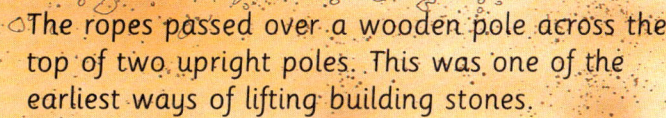

More about: forces pp8-9, 11  friction pp12-13  wheels pp18-23

# Levers

People have been using levers for thousands of years. A lever works like a see-saw.

If you sit on one end of a see-saw, the other end goes up.

A see-saw is balanced in the middle on an upright post called the pivot or **fulcrum**.

If you sit on one end of the see-saw and someone else sits on the other end, it will only balance if you are both the same weight.

If you are heavier than the other person, it will go down at your end.

You can only balance the see-saw if the heavier person sits nearer the middle.

Two people of the same weight balance the see-saw if they sit the same distance from the fulcrum.

If one person sits nearer the fulcrum, the see-saw will go down at the other end.

When you make the see-saw go up and down, you are using it as a lever to lift each other.

A lever has to have a fulcrum. You need less force or effort if the fulcrum is nearer the load and you have a long lever.

A person digging the garden uses a spade as a lever to lift soil. The handle is a long lever.

## Levers for throwing

A lever can make an object fly further or faster than throwing it by hand. Early weapons made use of levers.

### The mangonel
Stones were hurled by giant catapults pulled back by levers.

### The trebuchet
A heavy rock made one end go down, hurling a smaller rock on the other end through the air at the enemy.

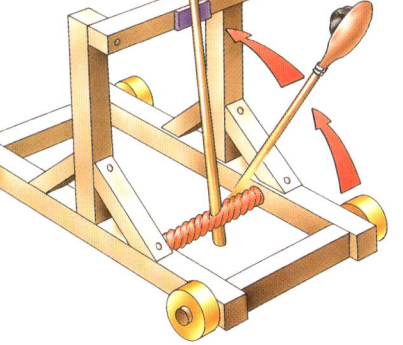

## Did you know...?

Archimedes was a mathematician in ancient Greece. He said that he could use a lever to move the Earth if only he had a fulcrum and somewhere to stand.

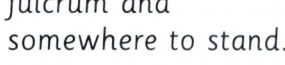

Balance a ruler on a pencil to make a see-saw. Find three 10p coins. Put one coin on each end of the ruler so that the see-saw balances. Move one coin halfway towards the pencil. What happens? Put the third coin on top of the one you just moved. Does the see-saw balance now? Move the coins nearer to the fulcrum. What happens?

Try to loosen a tin lid with a long spoon handle. Where is the fulcrum? Could you open the tin as easily with a shorter lever?

More about: forces pp8-9, 11, 15  simple machines pp18-19

# Gears

Gears consist of cogs of different sizes which work together. The cogs have teeth which may fit or **mesh** into the teeth on another cog. Bicycles and cars have gears like this.

Going downhill, gravity helps your bike go faster.

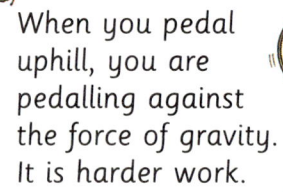

When you pedal uphill, you are pedalling against the force of gravity. It is harder work.

## Bicycle gears

Gears help you to make the most of your effort.

The pedals of a bike are connected to a large-toothed wheel or **cog**. A chain runs over this wheel and round a smaller cog on the back wheel.

As you pedal, the large pedal cog starts to turn and the chain makes the small cog on the wheel turn with it.

Suppose the large cog has four times as many teeth as the small cog. When the large cog turns once, the smaller cog turns four times.

## Car gears

A car engine has to work hard when the car starts to move or goes uphill. The driver chooses a low gear. As the car picks up speed or reaches the top of the hill, the driver changes to a higher gear.

## Changing direction

On some machines, gears change the direction of the force. The teeth of an upright or **vertical** wheel mesh into the teeth of a sideways or **horizontal** wheel.

An egg beater is a simple example. The handle turns a vertical wheel. This meshes with two small horizontal wheels which turn the blades of the beater.

Some mountain bikes have 12 gears or more. There are several cogs on the back wheel. The cyclist pushes a lever to move the chain from one cog to another.

More about: forces pp8-9, 11, 15   gravity pp8-9, 11   wheels pp14-15

# Using wind energy

Before coal and oil were widely used, people had to find other sources of energy to do jobs. They knew that the wind was strong enough to blow against the sails of a ship and move it through the water. By about 1150, people in Europe were using windmills to grind grain and pump water.

A windmill has large sails which are turned by the wind. If the sails point in only one direction, they would move only if the wind blows from the right direction. So the windmill has to be able to move to 'catch the wind'.

## Grinding mills

The sails are fixed to a horizontal pole or **shaft**. The shaft is connected by gear wheels to a vertical shaft. At the bottom of this shaft is a heavy millstone for grinding grain.

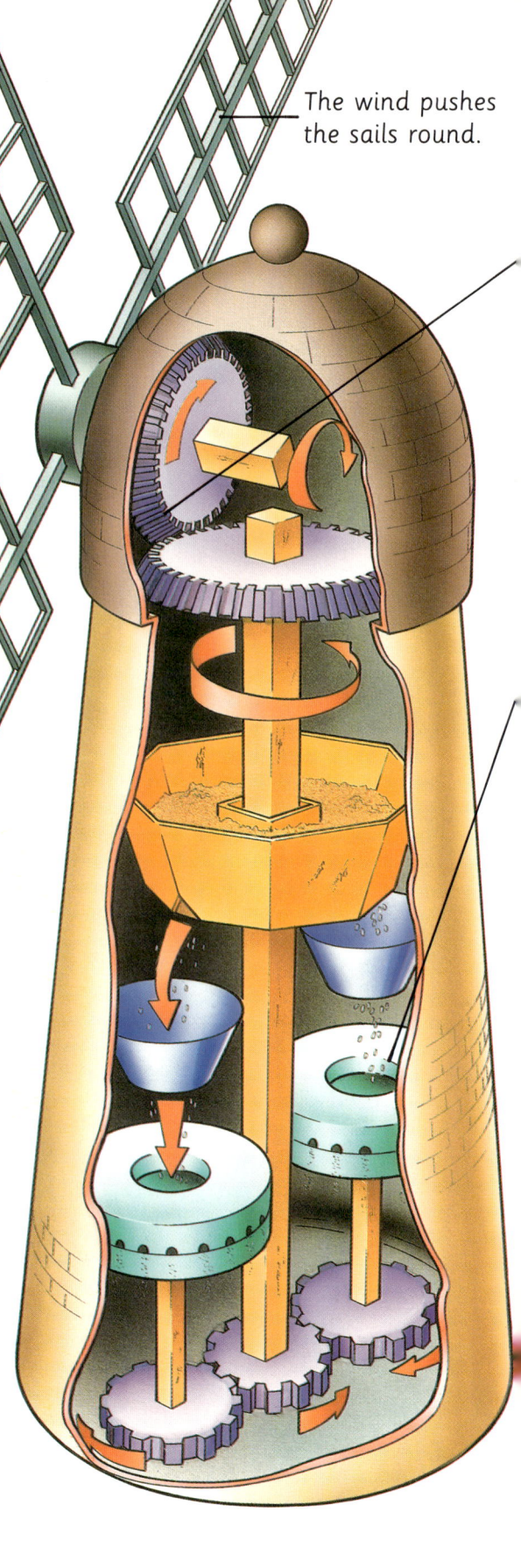

The wind pushes the sails round.

The horizontal shaft turns and the gear wheels change the direction of the force.

The vertical shaft turns the millstone which grinds against another heavy stone and crushes the grain into flour.

Most windmills are not used for grinding grain now, but many have been **restored**. Try to find out about one or visit it to see how it works.

The shafts of a windmill can also move a pump up and down to drain water from the land.

## Parachutes

Have you watched a parachutist drift to the ground? The parachute is shaped like a mushroom. It pushes against the air as it moves downwards. This causes friction which slows it down. Without the parachute, the person would plummet to the ground.

Some animals have folds of skin which act like parachutes. Flying squirrels can glide about 50 m. Flying lizards, geckos (another type of lizard) and frogs all use the same method.

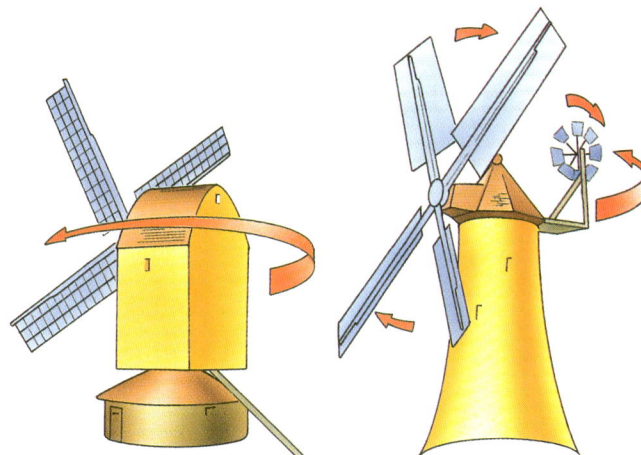

The German post mill is supported on a pole. The whole millhouse moves around this pole.

On a Dutch mill, the sails and roof move round.

The flying lemur, from South East Asia, has flaps of skin from its head to the end of its tail. It uses these to glide several hundred metres from tree to tree.

Find out more about these windmills in the Netherlands in the *New Horizons* book, *Land, water and air*.

More about: flying p9  wind energy pp11, 13

# Using water energy

If you try to row a boat against the flow of a river, you will know how strong the flow can be. Moving water has lots of energy.

A water wheel makes use of the moving energy of a river to drive machinery. Water wheels have been used for over 4000 years.

Find out more about spinning and weaving in the *New Horizons* book, *What is it made of?*

## The undershot wheel

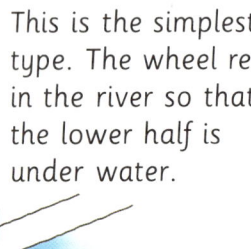

This is the simplest type. The wheel rests in the river so that the lower half is under water.

The flow of the river pushes the wheel round.

## How water wheels were used

Water wheels were connected to shafts which turned millstones to grind flour. They were also used to drive cloth-making machinery.

Until about 200 years ago, threads were spun and woven by hand which was very slow. The first spinning and weaving machines were turned by water power.

The cloth mill was built near a fast-flowing river.

## The overshot wheel

The water goes along a chute which ends above the top of the wheel.

Water drops from the chute on to one paddle after another and turns the wheel.

The overshot wheel turns faster than the undershot because it uses the moving and falling energy of the water.

Water **turbines** work in the same way as a water wheel, but they need more force than the flow of a river. A river is held back by a dam and forms a **reservoir**. When the gates in the dam are opened, the water rushes through and makes a turbine spin.

Each machine was connected to the driveshaft by wheels with a moving belt round them.

The belts took the energy from the shaft to the machines.

The shaft was connected by gear wheels to a horizontal shaft, called the driveshaft.

A water wheel was connected to a long vertical shaft.

## The use of steam

The first engines were driven by steam from boiling water. In 1712, Thomas Newcomen built a steam engine to pump water out of coal mines. Other **engineers**, such as James Watt, Richard Trevithick and George Stephenson, invented more efficient steam engines to drive factory machinery and the locomotives which pulled trains.

More about: coal mines pp26-27  gears pp18-19  turbines pp36-37

# How fuels formed

Coal, oil and gas are types of fuel. A fuel is a useful store of energy. **Fossil** fuels were formed from living things which died millions of years ago. A fossil is the remains of any plant or animal which lived in **prehistoric** times.

Find out more about fossils in two *New Horizons* books, *Life around us* and *Land, water and air*.

About 350 million years ago, parts of the Earth were covered with very wet, soft ground called swamps.

Dead plants rotted and changed into **peat**. Peat is used as a fuel in some places. It contains stored energy.

Forests of trees and giant ferns grew in the swamps.

Rivers brought more wet sand and mud.

When the trees and ferns died, they sank into the soft mud.

The rivers brought more mud to add to the layers.

More trees died and fell into the mud.

# Coal

Gradually, the peat sank deeper and deeper into the ground.

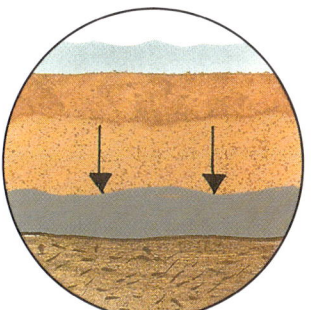

The mud and sand were **compressed** or pressed down tightly under more layers until they formed rock on top of the peat.

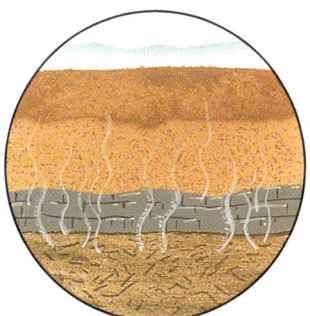

The pressure of the layers caused heat to build up.

This heat changed the peat into **seams** or layers of coal.

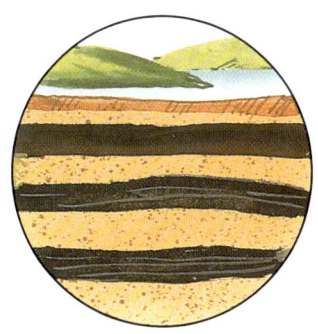

Layers of peat and coal built up for about 80 million years. Then, the swamps began to dry out.

# Oil and gas

When tiny animals and plants which lived in the seas died, they sank to the bottom. They were buried under layers of sand.

The compressed layers turned into rock. Heat gradually turned the remains of the animals and plants into oil.

Gases were produced by the **decaying** animals and plants. These gases were trapped in the rock with the oil.

More about: heat pp37, 40-41  rivers pp22-23  stored energy pp6-7

# Coal

Peat will change into coal only when it is compressed under many layers of rock. Most coal is buried deep in the ground. Before we can use it, we have to find it.

Power stations burn coal to produce electricity. Some are built near coal mines.

## Finding coal

**Geologists** study the layers of rock under the surface. First, they make a **survey** or close study of an area. Sometimes they set off small explosions. The sound travels through the rocks and bounces back. The time it takes to bounce back depends on the types of rock it travels through.

Next, they make a test drilling. A hollow pipe is drilled through the rocks. It brings up a sample of all the rock layers.

## Mining for coal

The coal seam may be 5 km under the surface.

The tunnels become longer as more coal is cut. Miners may be working several kilometres from the shafts.

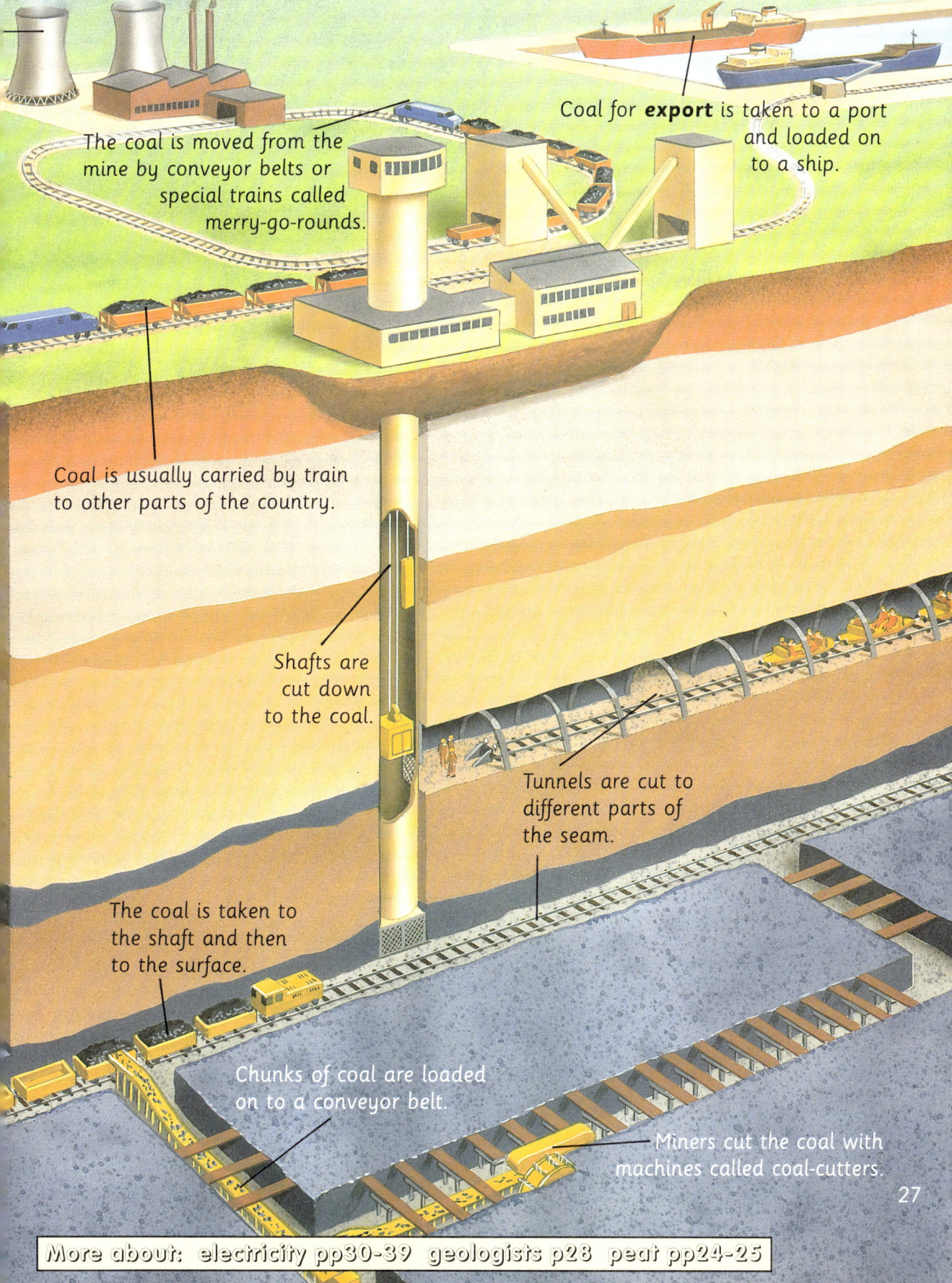

The coal is moved from the mine by conveyor belts or special trains called merry-go-rounds.

Coal for **export** is taken to a port and loaded on to a ship.

Coal is usually carried by train to other parts of the country.

Shafts are cut down to the coal.

Tunnels are cut to different parts of the seam.

The coal is taken to the shaft and then to the surface.

Chunks of coal are loaded on to a conveyor belt.

Miners cut the coal with machines called coal-cutters.

More about: electricity pp30-39  geologists p28  peat pp24-25

# Oil and gas

When oil and gas formed millions of years ago, more of the Earth was covered by seas than it is today. This means that oil and gas can be found on land as well as under the sea.

Oil and gas are found in soft rock under layers of hard rock. Oil can flow through the soft rock, but the hard rock stops it.

When geologists think they have found oil, a well is drilled.

A steel tower called a derrick supports the drilling equipment.

An oil company may drill hundreds of wells on an oilfield.

The drill is made up of lengths of pipe with a cutting part called the 'bit' on the end.

More lengths of pipe are added as the drill bores into the ground.

Sometimes the rock forms a dome over the soft rock. The oil is pushed upwards, but the hard dome traps it. The push from underground may be strong enough to send oil gushing to the surface and keep it flowing through the pipeline.
Sometimes oil has to be pumped out.

Natural gas is often found in the same places as oil. It is piped to the surface in the same way.

Oil is carried by pipeline to a **refinery**. There it is turned into petrol, diesel and other oil products.

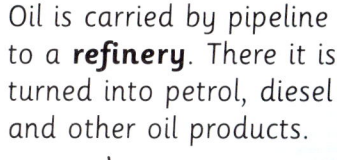

Then, the gas is carried by pipeline to a gas plant where it is treated to make it safe to use.

## Finding oil and gas at sea

Oil companies also drill for oil and gas under the sea bed. A platform called an oil rig holds the drilling equipment and the workers. A massive pipeline is laid along the sea bed to carry the oil or gas from the rig to the shore.

More about: gas pp25, 30-31   geologists p26   oil pp25, 30-31

# Using fuels

Imagine what the world would be like without coal, oil and gas.

Power stations burn coal, oil or gas to make electricity.

Some houses are heated by oil-fired, gas-fired, electricity or coal-powered central heating. Others use open fires.

Streets can be lit by electric lights.

Some houses have a gas cooker, others have electric cookers or microwave ovens.

Petrol and diesel are products of oil. Think how many cars and lorries could not run without these fuels.

Plastics and fertilisers are made from substances which come from oil.

Gas is a useful and efficient fuel, but it can explode or it can suffocate you if you breathe it in. Natural gas does not smell, so people may not realise if there is a gas leak. As this could be very dangerous, a smell is added to the gas at the gas plant.

Many trains run on electricity. Farmers use fuel oil for their machines and electricity to work their milking machines. Can you think of other uses for fuels?

## Oil products

Oil straight from the ground is called **crude oil**. Before it can be used, it has to be separated into different parts, then treated to clean it and remove dangerous gases. This happens at the refinery. The separate parts are shown in the diagram on the right.

petroleum gas

petrol

kerosene

diesel oil

lubricants

fuel oil

bitumen

Find out more about oil products in the *New Horizons* book, *What is it made of?*

More about: fuels pp4-5, 24-29, 38-39  generating electricity pp34-37

# Electricity

Electricity was discovered more than 2000 years ago by the ancient Greeks. They found that if a stone called amber was rubbed against certain types of cloth such as silk, bits of dust and straw were **attracted** to the stone. They stuck to it because of **static electricity**, caused by friction.

## Did you know...?

- The word 'electricity' comes from 'elektron' which is the Greek word for amber.
- The first person to make a battery was an Italian named Alessandro Volta (1745–1827). The energy carried by an electric current is measured in volts.

In 1752, an American, Benjamin Franklin, discovered that there are two types of electric charge.

He called these positive (+) and negative (−) charges.

Opposite charges attract each other.

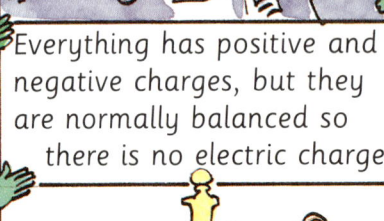

Everything has positive and negative charges, but they are normally balanced so there is no electric charge.

If something happens to change this balance, then the object will have more of one type of charge.

Try this test. Comb your hair for about 1 minute. Hold the comb above your head. What happens? During combing, friction causes some of the negative charge from your hair to pass into the comb. This leaves your hair with a positive charge, and the comb with a negative charge. Opposite charges attract, so your hair is attracted to the comb.

Rub your comb or a blown-up balloon against a woollen sweater. Now try to pick up some small pieces of paper with the comb or balloon. What happens?

## Electric batteries

The word static means 'stay still'. The charges in static electricity do not move. They are made to flow in an electric **current** – a moving charge. Metals are good **conductors** of electricity, so electricity can pass along metal wires.

A battery gives the charge energy and makes it move. One part of a battery has a negative charge. The other part has a positive charge. The negative charge is attracted to the positive charge. If wires are attached to both parts and connected to a light bulb, they form a continuous **circuit**. The current can move along the wires. Energy is transferred from the current to the bulb and it lights up.

During a thunderstorm, the moving air separates out the charges in the clouds.

Positive charges build up in the top.

Negative charges build up in the bottom.

Negative charges are attracted to positive charges on the ground.

They jump to Earth or to other clouds as a huge electric charge or flash of lightning.

Lightning is so powerful that it can kill people if it strikes them.

More about: attraction pp34-35   electricity pp30-31, 34-39

# Magnets and electricity

**Magnetism** is a force which occurs between some metals. Iron, steel nickel and cobalt are magnetic metals. A magnet will pick up an iron nail, but it will not pick up an aluminium can. Aluminium is non-magnetic.

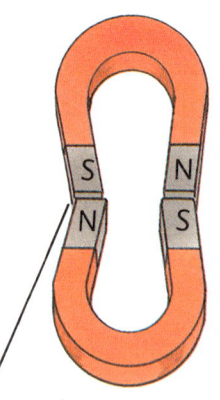

If you put them together like this, they will push apart.

Magnets have two **poles**. If you put them together like this, they will attract each other.

The British scientist William Gilbert (1544–1603) studied magnetism. He suggested that the Earth behaves like a giant magnet. Other magnets always point to the Earth's poles.

The iron at the centre of the Earth makes it act like a magnet. If you hang a bar magnet from a piece of string, its north pole will swing round to point to Earth's North Pole.

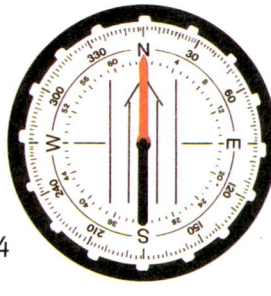

A compass needle is a tiny magnet. It swings round to point to magnetic north. You use a compass to see what direction you are going in.

34

## The link with magnets

In 1819, Danish scientist Hans Oersted found that an electric current flowing along a wire made a compass needle turn. The electric current made the wire behave like a magnet.

In 1831, British scientist Michael Faraday used a magnet to produce electricity.

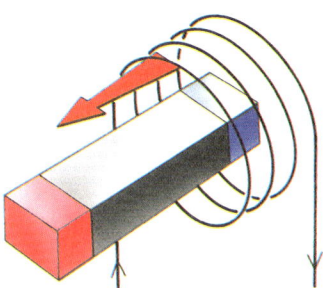

He moved a loop of wire over a magnet and an electric current flowed in the wire.

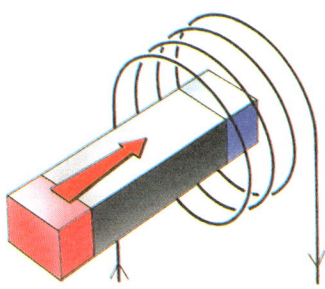

He discovered that the same thing happened if he kept the wire still and moved the magnet.

## Electric motors

An electric motor transfers energy from an electric current into moving energy. A coil of wire is placed between the two poles of a magnet. An electric current is sent through the wire. It makes the wire act like another magnet. The poles of the ordinary magnet push away from the poles of the wire magnet. This makes the coil spin round and turn the motor.

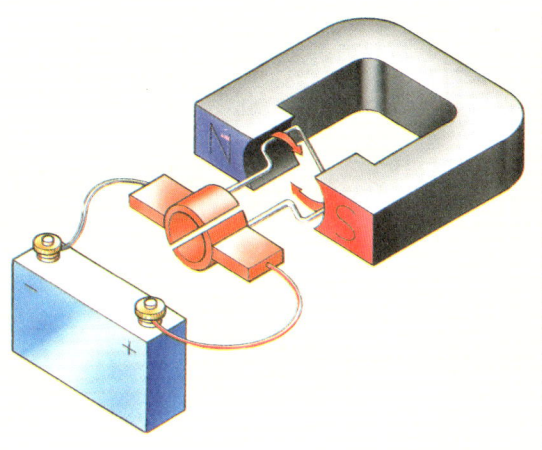

### Did you know...?

About 2500 years ago, the Chinese discovered that a black stone, called lodestone, attracted small pieces of iron. A piece of lodestone hung on a string swung round to point north. Sailors used lodestone as the first compasses.

Make your own magnet. Rub an iron nail against a magnet. The nail becomes a magnet itself. Try lifting steel paper clips or pins with your new magnet.
Use your magnet to pick up different types of metal. Which metals are magnetic?

More about: attraction pp32-33  electric currents p33

# Generating electricity

Power stations still use Faraday's method to **generate** or produce electricity. He was transferring the energy from his body to turn the wire. This produced only a small amount of energy carried by the electricity.

Power stations produce huge amounts of energy using a machine called a generator. The energy is carried by the electric current so we can use it easily.

## Inside a power station

Coal, oil or gas are burned to boil water to make steam.
The steam rushes through pipes and turns a wheel with blades, called a turbine.

The covers of this turbo-generator have been removed. Can you see the rows of blades?

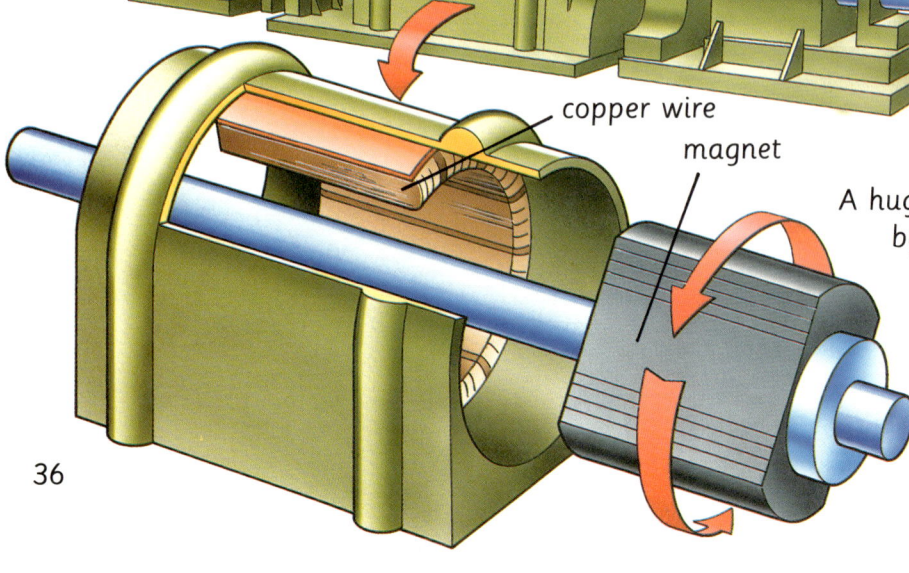

The turbine is connected to the generator by a shaft.

copper wire
magnet

A huge magnet is surrounded by a coil of copper wire.

As the turbine spins, the magnet spins and produces an electric current in the wire.

# Other ways of generating electricity

Many people are worried about what will happen when coal, oil and gas run out. The **pollution** caused by burning fuels is another problem. Many countries use **nuclear fuels** to generate electricity. Some people are worried about the pollution caused by nuclear power plants. Electricity can also be generated using **renewable** energy sources, like the wind and flowing water. These will not run out. The moving energy of the wind or water is transferred to a turbine.

Wind turbines act like windmills. The blade must spin round very fast, so there has to be a strong wind.

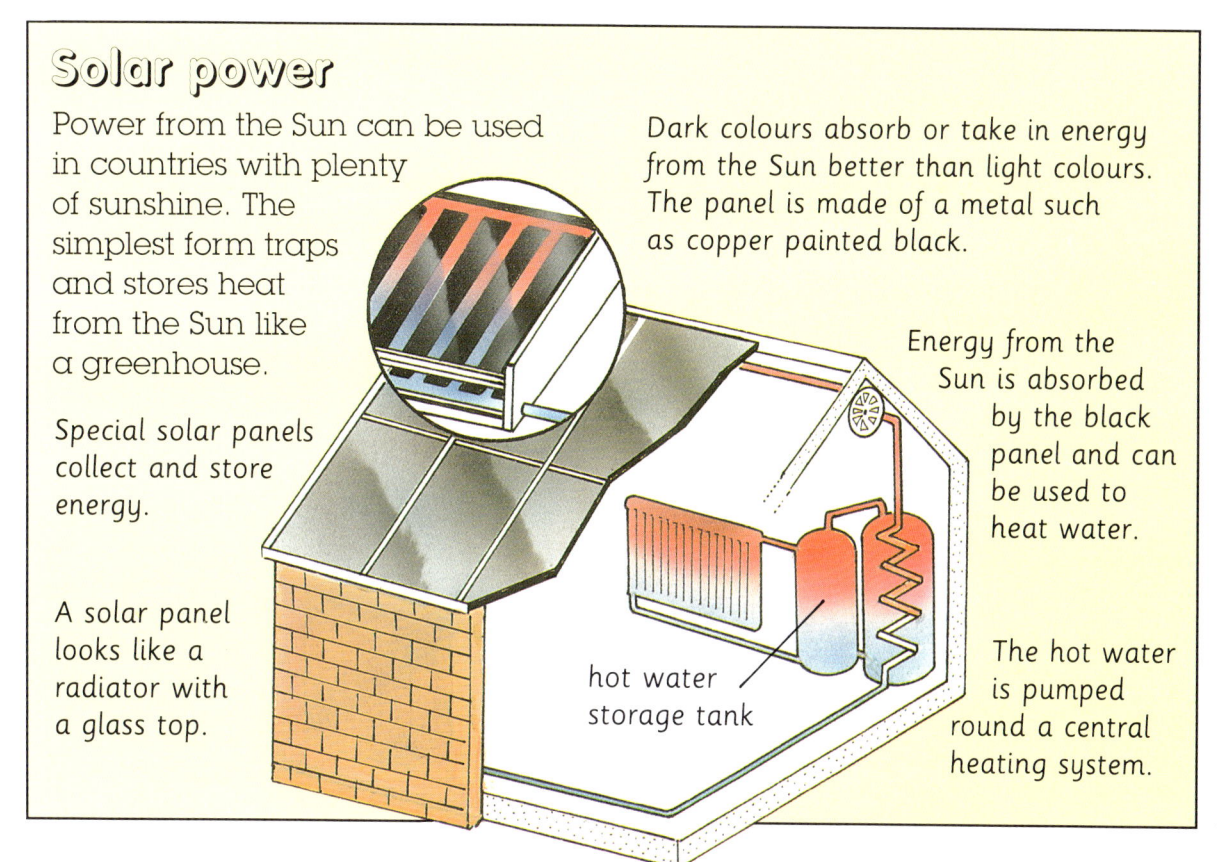

## Solar power

Power from the Sun can be used in countries with plenty of sunshine. The simplest form traps and stores heat from the Sun like a greenhouse.

Special solar panels collect and store energy.

A solar panel looks like a radiator with a glass top.

Dark colours absorb or take in energy from the Sun better than light colours. The panel is made of a metal such as copper painted black.

Energy from the Sun is absorbed by the black panel and can be used to heat water.

hot water storage tank

The hot water is pumped round a central heating system.

More about: heating pp40-41  water turbines p23  windmills pp20-21

# Carrying electricity and gas

Smaller cables and pipes lead from the mains to houses and other buildings.

The big electricity cables and gas pipelines are called the mains supplies.

Electricity cables and gas pipes are buried in trenches under the ground.

Thick wires, or cables, strung between **pylons** carry electricity from power stations to wherever it is needed.

Overhead cables are the cheapest way of carrying electricity, but they cannot always be used. There is no room for pylons in the middle of a town.

If there is a gas leak, workers have to dig under the roads to mend the pipe.

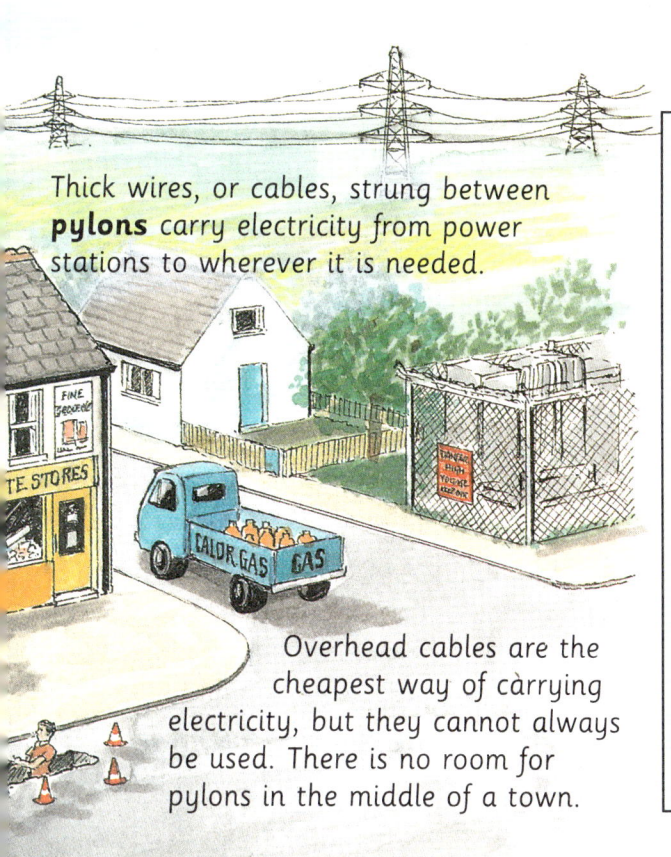

Bad weather can bring cables down. This may cut off the electricity supply to thousands of people at a time. In 1987, a hurricane hit Britain. Some towns and villages were without electricity for days.

## Controlling the supply

Gas can be stored until it is needed, but there is no easy way of storing energy as electricity. Power stations have to produce the amount people need, when they need it. When it is dark and cold, people use more electricity for lights and fires. When people watch television, they often make a hot drink halfway through a programme, or at the end. If a lot of people do this at the same time, there is a sudden need for more electricity.

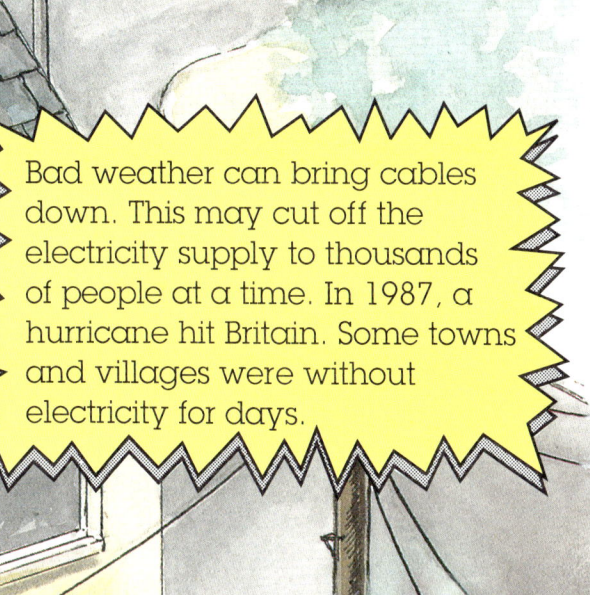

The cables from power stations are linked up all over the country to form one big supply system, or **grid**. Electricity can be sent to any part of the country as it is needed.

More about: electricity pp30-37   gas pp25, 30-31   using fuels pp30-31

# Heat

When a fuel burns, the energy heats up the air and spreads out. Hot objects have more energy than cold objects.

Snow and ice are formed when water freezes and becomes solid. Frozen water (ice) has less energy than liquid water.

When ice is heated, it is given more energy which makes it melt, or turn back into liquid water.

## Conduction

Energy can travel in solids. If you leave a spoon standing in boiling water, the end becomes hot.

Metals are good conductors of energy – the energy moves along them easily.

The energy moves along the spoon. This is called **conduction**.

## Convection

When liquids and gases get hot, they expand.

When the Sun shines on rivers, lakes and seas, the water heats up and **evaporates** (turns into water vapour).

The vapour rises, cools and forms clouds of water droplets. The drops fall to the Earth as rain.

This is known as the **water cycle**. Find out more about it in the *New Horizons* book, *Land, water and air*.

If the water is given more energy, it gets hotter, boils and turns into water vapour.

Energy has changed the solid into a liquid and then into a gas.

When you take your temperature, the level of the liquid in the thermometer shows the temperature of your body. Do you know what body temperature is, normally?

## Measuring temperature

Wood is not a good conductor. A wooden handle on a metal spoon slows down the movement of the energy.

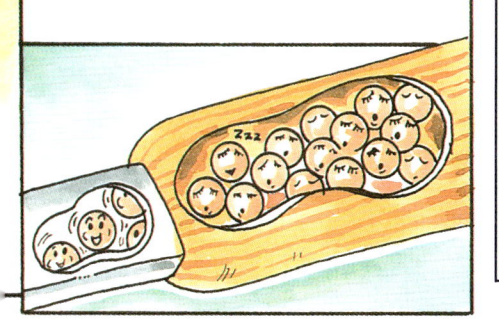

**Temperature** is the measurement of 'hotness'. It is measured using a thermometer. One type is a glass tube with temperatures marked on it. There is liquid in the bulb – either mercury or coloured alcohol. Mercury is a silver-coloured metal which is liquid at room temperature. As the liquid heats up, it expands and rises up the tube.

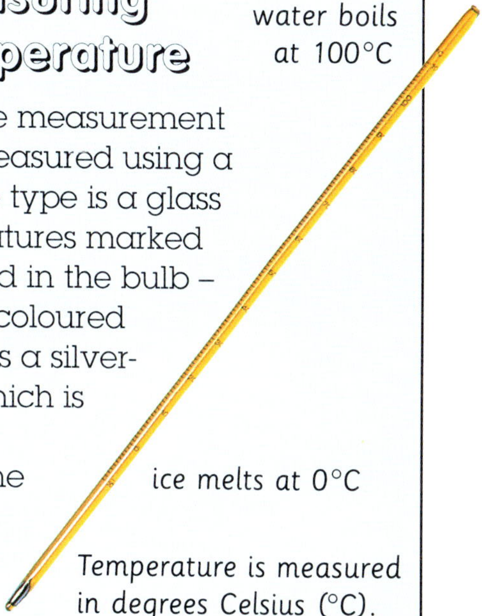

water boils at 100°C

ice melts at 0°C

Temperature is measured in degrees Celsius (°C).

When you heat water in a pan, the water at the bottom of the pan becomes hotter first.

It expands and rises, and cooler water moves in to take its place. This is called a **convection current**.

Energy from the Sun has to reach the Earth through space. The energy is in invisible rays, called infrared rays.

Light rays from the Sun also carry energy.

More about: gas pp25, 30-31, 38-39  light pp42-47  moving energy p7

# Light

We could not see without light. Daylight comes from the Sun. Light such as sunlight is known as white light.

Find out more about shadows in the *New Horizons* book, *Land, water and air*.

It cannot pass through **opaque** objects such as wood, or your body. The Sun's rays cannot bend to go round your body, so a shadow is cast on the ground.

Light travels in straight lines which can pass through empty spaces and **transparent** objects such as glass.

Some objects are **translucent**. They let in light, but you cannot see through them clearly.

Light is **reflected** from all the things you look at. It bounces back into your eyes, so that you can see things.

Find out more about how you see in the *New Horizons* book, *Look you! Look me!*

## Making white light

Red, green and blue are called the primary colours of light. If lights of these colours are mixed together, they make white light.

# The spectrum

In 1666, British scientist Sir Isaac Newton showed that white light can be split into seven colours. You can see these colours in a rainbow. Red, orange, yellow, green, blue, indigo and violet are the colours of the **spectrum**.

You often see a rainbow when the Sun shines while it is raining. The drops of water bend the rays of light from the Sun into separate colours.

## Did you know...?

Light waves travel at 300 000 km/s (kilometres per second). The Sun is 150 million km from the Earth, so a light wave takes about 8 minutes to travel from the Sun to the Earth. Scientists believe that nothing can travel faster than light.

## Making a rainbow

You can make a rainbow using a triangular glass block called a prism. A prism acts like a raindrop. The light rays bend and split into the colours of the spectrum. Each colour bends a slightly different amount.

You cannot see light. Test this by shining a torch in a darkened room. Objects in the room reflect the torch light, so you can see them. You can see the light from the torch only if there is dust in the air. The bits of dust reflect some of the light into your eyes.

More about: reflection p44   refraction p45   Sun's rays p37

# Bouncing light

When light falls on an opaque surface, some is absorbed and some is reflected. Black surfaces absorb most of the light. Rough surfaces absorb more light than smooth surfaces.

Light passes through shiny transparent surfaces such as water and glass, but some of it is bounced back or reflected.

White surfaces reflect light. Why are these buildings in Portugal painted white?

## Mirrors

One side of a sheet of glass is painted silver. The paint stops any light passing through the glass. When you look in a mirror, your reflection seems to be back to front.

Shiny surfaces reflect the most light. A mirror reflects all the light that falls on it.

Look into the flat surface of a pond. What can you see reflected?

44

# Bending light

Light rays bend when they pass from one type of transparent substance to another. For example, they bend when they pass from air into water. Bending of light is called **refraction**.

Hold a straight straw in water. Refraction of light makes the straw look bent. Light travels fast through the air, but water slows it down.

## Changing your image

Mirrors and lenses can be curved in different ways to alter how you see.

Look at your reflection in the back of a shiny spoon. The curve of the spoon reflects more objects than a flat mirror would.

Mirrors which curve outwards like this are called **convex** mirrors.

The front of the spoon curves inwards. It is a **concave** mirror.

Concave mirrors sometimes make things look bigger. Shaving mirrors are often concave.

## Seeing in the dark

Cats' eyes have special reflectors at the back. These reflectors can collect light, even if it is very dim.

A cat's pupils open wide in dim light.

They close to narrow slits when light is bright, so the cat is not dazzled.

### Did you know...?

Cat's eyes gave Percy Shaw the idea for the reflecting road studs which mark the centre of some roads. He invented them in 1934.

More about: light rays pp42-43, 46-47   mirrors p47   refraction pp43, 46-47

# How you see

Light enters your eye through the **pupil**.

A clear, curved piece of jelly, called the **lens**, bends the light to **focus** the picture on the back of your eye.

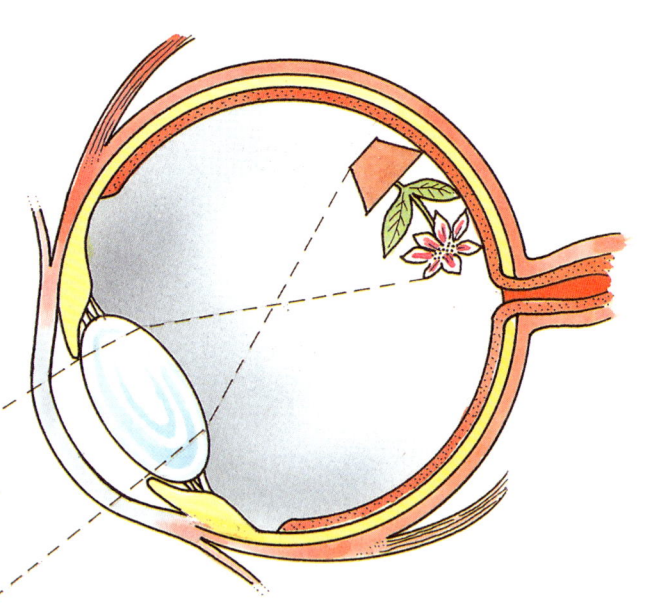

A clear, sharp, but upside-down picture falls on your **retina**. Your brain corrects it, so that you see everything the right way up.

## Improving sight

Some people cannot see clearly because the lenses in their eyes do not focus the light on the retina. They see a blurred picture. Some lenses can be used to correct poor sight.

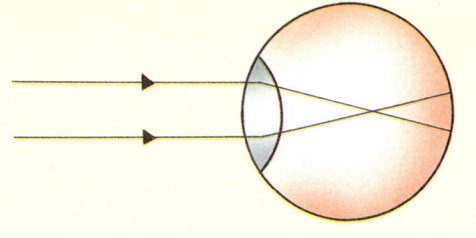

Short-sighted people cannot see distant objects clearly. The lens focusses the picture in front of the retina.

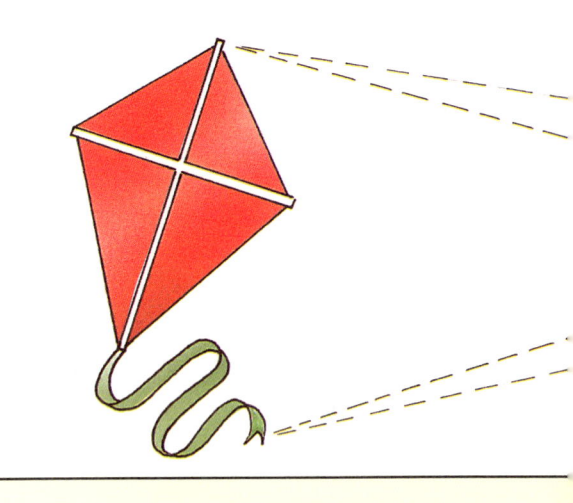

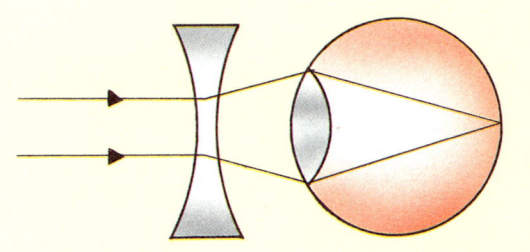

Short-sight is corrected with a concave lens.

A magnifying glass is a convex lens which bends light rays inwards. Objects look much larger when seen through the glass.

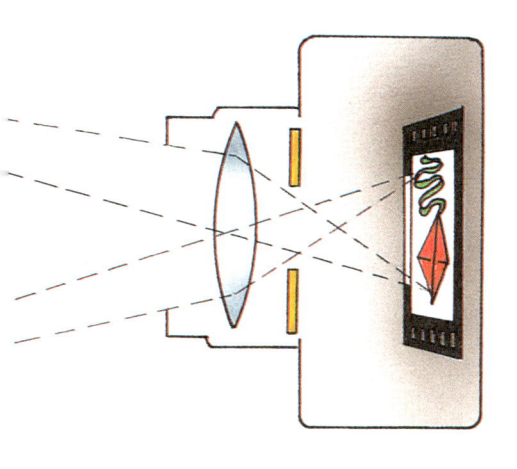

The lens in a camera works in a similar way to the lens in your eye. A piece of curved glass bends light rays to focus a picture on the film.

Telescopes and microscopes make things look very much larger. They use a more complicated system of mirrors and lenses. The telescope in the picture is used for looking at distant stars and planets. Its mirror measures 272 cm across.

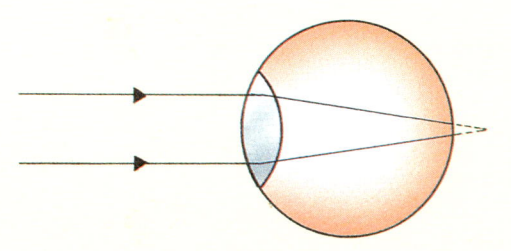

Long-sighted people cannot see close objects clearly. The lens focusses the picture behind the retina.

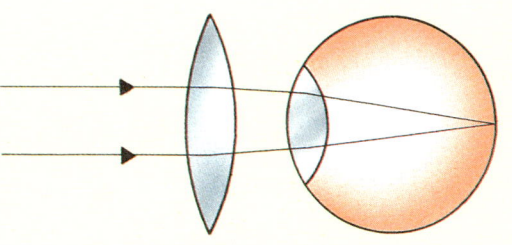

Long-sight is corrected with a convex lens.

47

More about: reflection pp42, 44  refraction pp43, 45

# Sound

We use sound to communicate with people and understand what is going on around us. All sounds are made by very rapid movements or **vibrations**.

As you talk to your friend, the vocal cords at the top of your windpipe vibrate.

When the sound waves vibrate against your friend's eardrums, your friend hears what you are saying.

Find out more about talking and hearing in the *New Horizons* book, *Look you! Look me!*

The vibrations pass through the air as sound waves.

Sound travels through air. It also travels through other materials.

Thicker, softer materials tend to absorb some of the sound. You cannot hear it so well.

Sound waves bounce off hard surfaces. This causes an echo. You hear the sound as it is made, then again as it bounces back to you.

## Loud and soft sounds

If you drop a stone into a pond, ripples spread across the surface. Sound waves spread out like ripples as they vibrate through the air. They become weaker the further they travel. A whisper causes a gentle ripple. The sound waves do not travel far. A loud noise causes a strong ripple.

Sometimes sound vibrations are so violent, they can damage your eardrums.

### Did you know...?
Sound travels through air at about 1200 km/h. During a storm, do you hear the thunder or see the lightning first? Why?

Sound vibrations must travel through something. In space there is no air, so sound cannot travel. Astronauts have to speak to each other by radio. Radio waves can travel in space.

## How other animals use sound

Bats cannot see well. They fly at night using echoes to avoid bumping into things and to find food. Bats give out a very high-pitched sound, which bounces off the objects around it. The echo tells the bat where and what the object is.

The male tree frog sings to attract a female. The sounds vibrate in a bag like a balloon on its throat.

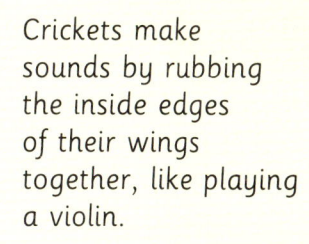

Crickets make sounds by rubbing the inside edges of their wings together, like playing a violin.

49

More about: lightning p33  radio pp56-57  reflection pp42, 44

# Recording sound

Sound can be recorded on tape, on flat discs or records. First, the sound is turned into electrical signals by a microphone.

A small piece of metal moves backwards and forwards as the sound waves hit it.

A small coil of wire, attached to the metal, also moves with the sound waves.

Near the coil, a magnet produces an electric current in the moving wire.

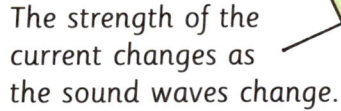

The strength of the current changes as the sound waves change.

This pattern of currents or signals is passed into a machine which records them on tape or on a record.

### Did you know...?
- An American, Thomas Edison, invented the phonograph – the first record player – in 1877.
- The first musical recording is thought to have been made in 1878 in New York.

## Recording on tape

The record head in a tape recorder is a special magnet. The tape is a thin ribbon of plastic which has been covered with fine iron dust. The tape moves past the record head, where electric currents magnetise the iron dust into the pattern of the sounds. When the tape is played back, the pattern is turned back into an electrical signal and then into sound.

The pattern of iron particles on blank tape.

The pattern of iron particles on recorded tape.

## Recording on disc

A pointed cutter makes a groove in a metal disc. Electrical signals guide the cutter to cut the groove in the pattern of the original sounds. Plastic copies of the record are made for sale.

Compact discs are made in a similar way. Instead of a cutter, electrical signals guide an intense beam of light called a **laser**. The laser cuts the pattern of sounds into the disc.

More about: magnets pp34-35 recording p59 sound waves pp48-49, 56-57

# Sending messages by wire

Today, you can pick up the telephone and talk to someone on the other side of the world. Before the telegraph was invented, people had to write letters or travel long distances to keep in touch.

## The telegraph

In 1837, an American, Samuel Morse, invented the electric telegraph. This was the first way of using electricity to send messages along wires. Morse used a code system of long buzzes (dashes) and short buzzes (dots) to stand for the letters of the alphabet. Specially-trained operators tapped out a message at one end. A buzzer sounded at the other end, and another operator decoded the message.

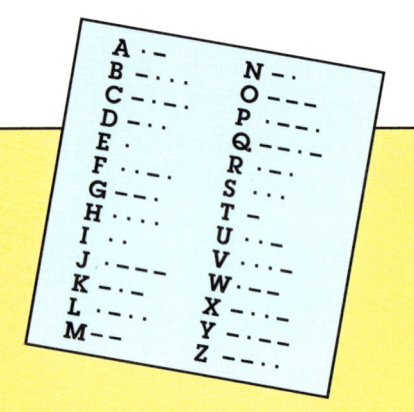

The telegraph also printed out the coded message on a strip of paper.

## The modern telegraph

A telex is a sort of telegraph.

People with telex have their own special number, like a telephone number. They also need a telephone, a printer and a typewriter.

The operator dials the telex number to link up with the person at the other end.

Fax is an even more modern way of sending messages along wires. The print on letters and other papers, and pictures can be turned into electrical signals and sent to someone along telephone wires.

A fax receiver at the other end turns the signals back into copies of the papers.

> What would your name look like in Morse code? Make up a message and see if your friends can work it out. Now try to tap out a message!

The message is typed on the typewriter. It is turned into electrical signals which travel along the telephone wires.

At the other end, the signals are turned back into words and printed out on the printer.

More about: electrical signals pp50-51, 54-61 telephone pp54-55

# The telephone

The telephone was invented in 1876 by Alexander Graham Bell, a Scot who taught deaf children to speak in the USA. His interest in speech and sounds gave him the idea.

## Bell's telephone

Bell made a **transmitter** which had a disc that vibrated like the eardrum. A transmitter sends out sound messages. The transmitter was linked by wire to a receiver which also had a vibrating disc. When someone spoke into the transmitter, the disc vibrated. The sound vibrations were passed along the wire as electrical signals. The receiver picked them up with its vibrating disc and changed them back into words.

A microphone changes sounds into electrical signals.

The signals are sent along wires to the earpiece of the other telephone.

mouthpiece

## The telephone today

The handset has an earpiece where you listen and a mouthpiece where you speak.

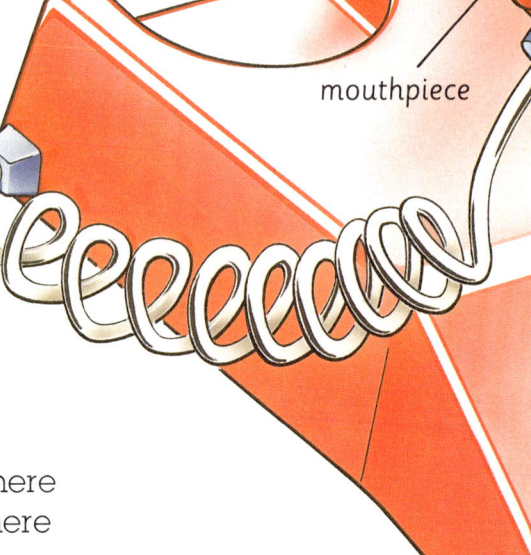

earpiece

loudspeaker

A loudspeaker changes electrical signals into sounds.

magnet

Coils of wire move as the signals pass through them.

They are attached to a thin piece of metal which also moves and makes the air vibrate. We hear these vibrations as sounds.

### Did you know...?
There are about 350 million telephones in the world.

### Telephones around the world

The wires from each telephone run to main cables. These cables run to the **exchange**. Calls are usually linked by computers. You can dial straight through to most places in the world.

More about: electrical signals pp50-53, 56-61  sound vibrations pp48-49

# Sending messages without wires

How does the sound from a radio station reach your radio when there is no wire between them? Sounds can be sent without wires. They travel through the air on **electromagnetic waves**.

## Sending messages by radio

You need a transmitter to send radio messages and a receiver to receive them.

### Did you know...?

Electromagnetic waves travel through space at about 300 000 km/s. Radio waves travel as fast as light (also an electromagnetic wave) and much faster than sound.

They spread out as electromagnetic radio waves.

In the transmitter, a microphone changes sounds into electrical signals.

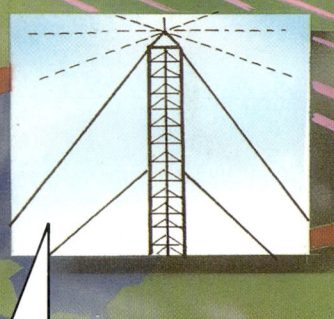

The signals pass to the **aerial** in the transmitter.

The waves are turned back into sounds by a loudspeaker in the receiver.

56

# The uses of radio

Radio provides news and entertainment, but it has other uses, too. The police, ambulance and other emergency services have radios so that they can keep in touch with their headquarters.

Aircraft have radios so that pilots can send and receive messages from airports.

The receiver needs an aerial to pick up radio waves.

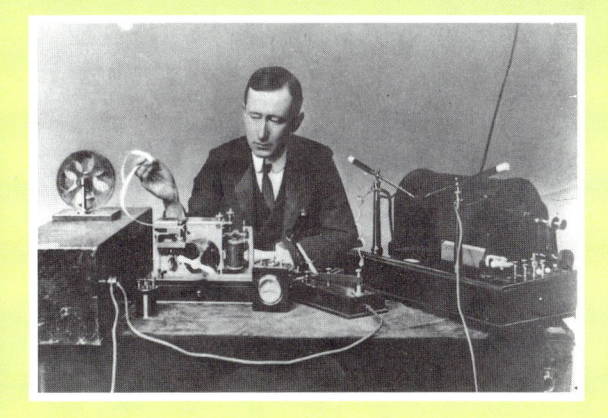

# The invention of radio

Radio was invented by an Italian, Guglielmo Marconi. In 1894, he began to experiment with electromagnetic waves. He called them 'wireless' waves.

In 1901, Marconi sent the first radio message across the Atlantic Ocean. After that, ships began to use radio regularly. Can you find out more about early radio? How is it used today?

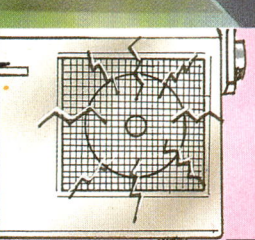

More about: electromagnetic waves pp58-59  light pp42-47

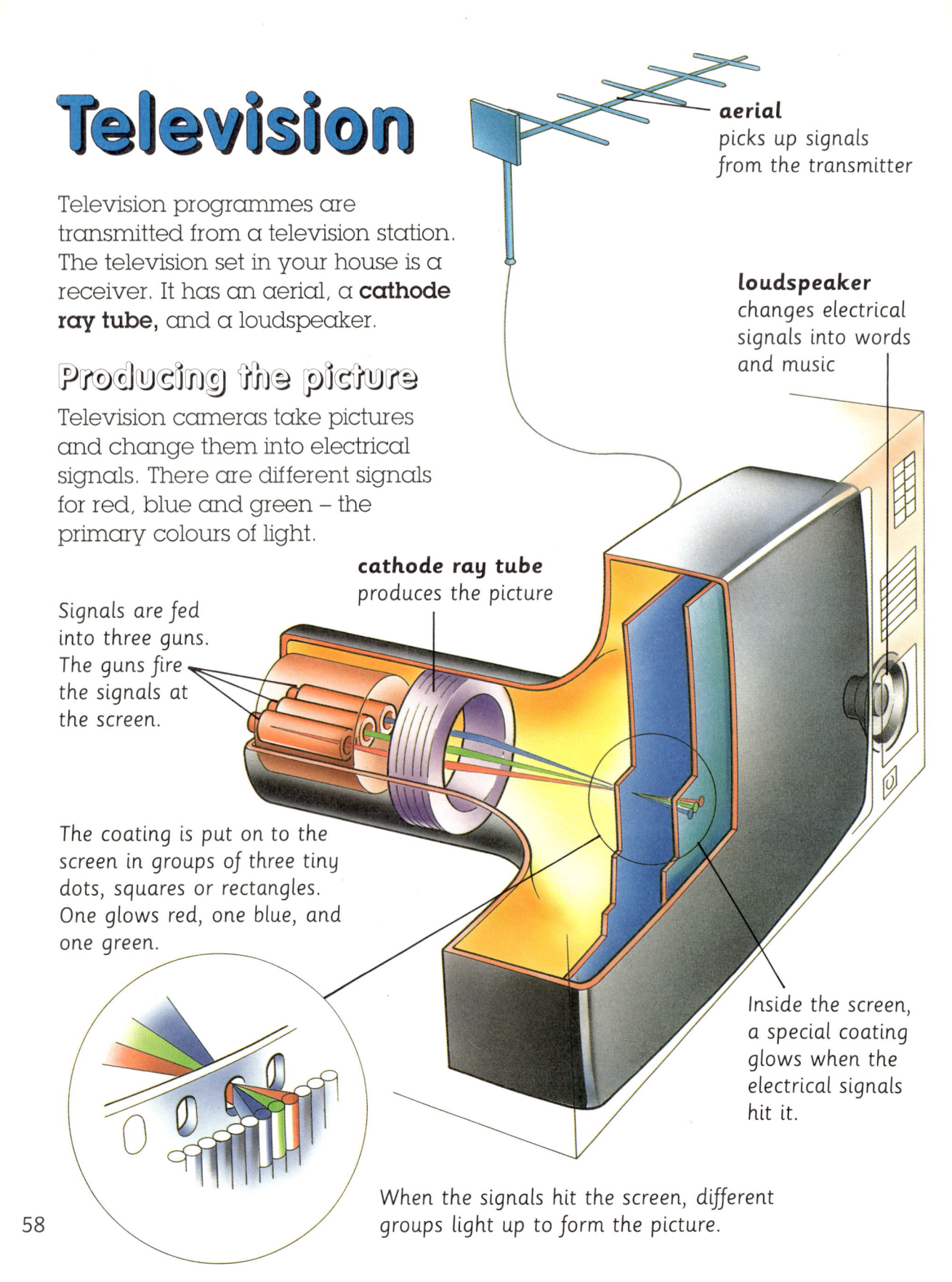

# Television

Television programmes are transmitted from a television station. The television set in your house is a receiver. It has an aerial, a **cathode ray tube,** and a loudspeaker.

## Producing the picture

Television cameras take pictures and change them into electrical signals. There are different signals for red, blue and green – the primary colours of light.

Signals are fed into three guns. The guns fire the signals at the screen.

The coating is put on to the screen in groups of three tiny dots, squares or rectangles. One glows red, one blue, and one green.

**aerial**
picks up signals from the transmitter

**loudspeaker**
changes electrical signals into words and music

**cathode ray tube**
produces the picture

Inside the screen, a special coating glows when the electrical signals hit it.

When the signals hit the screen, different groups light up to form the picture.

## The first television

In 1923, John Logie Baird, a Scottish inventor, thought of a way to transmit pictures using radio waves. He showed his first television pictures in 1926. Can you find out more about Baird's television? How was it different from television today?

## Storing pictures

A video recorder records pictures and sound. Electrical signals are turned into a magnetic pattern on the tape. When the tape is played, the magnetic pattern turns back into electrical signals. These are received by the television set and turned into pictures and sound.

Television crews use video camera recorders to collect news. Why is this quicker than using an ordinary camera and film?

## Satellites

Live programmes from other countries can be relayed by a satellite above the Earth.

The ground station transmits the signals to a satellite.

The satellite relays the signals to a ground station in another country.

Some people have a special satellite 'dish' aerial. They can pick up programme signals direct from satellites.

The programme signals are transmitted from the television station to a ground station.

The signals are transmitted to a television station and the programme is transmitted into people's homes.

More about: magnetic tape pp50-51 radio waves pp56-57

# Computers

Computers work things out very quickly and store information. They have replaced typewriters and filing cabinets in many offices. Letters, documents and information are typed into the computer using a keyboard. The computer has a separate printer which prints out the finished documents. Letters, documents and information can be stored on discs until they are needed again.

Offices of the future may have no paper in them at all. Everyone would have a computer screen and keyboard, a telephone and a modem. This is called a work station.

All the work stations in an office and in people's homes would be linked together.

Shops and factories store information about their stock in computers. Offices and banks store information about customers such as their address and their account details.

Computers are used in other ways, too. Can you find out about some of these? The pictures may give you clues.

A modem changes signals from a computer into signals that can be sent along telephone wires.

All messages would be sent by computer and telephone.

They would also be linked to a central computer which would store all the information about the business.

Modems would form links with people outside the office, and offices in other countries.

61

More about: electrical signals pp50-59 telephone wires pp52-55

# Key words

The meanings of words can depend on how and when they are used. You may find that as you learn more about science the meanings change slightly.

**acceleration** getting faster

**aerial** the part of a radio or television transmitter from which radio waves are sent into the air. The part of a radio or television receiver which picks up radio waves

**attraction** a force which draws two things together

**axle** the rod on which a wheel turns

**carbon dioxide** one of the gases in air

**cathode ray tube** the part of a television set which produces the picture

**circuit** the continuous path of an electric current

**cog** a wheel with teeth round the edge

**compressed** squeezed tightly together

**concave** curving inwards, like the bowl of a spoon

**conduction** the movement of energy through a solid

**conductor** a substance that allows energy to travel through it

**convection current** the movement of energy through a liquid or gas by the movement of the liquid or gas itself

**convex** curving outwards like the back of a spoon

**crude oil** oil as it is when it comes out of the ground

**current** a flow of electricity

**decay** to rot

**displace** to take the place of something else

**electric charge** the amount of electricity

**electromagnetic waves** waves which can travel through space

**energy** the ability to do a job

**engineer** someone who designs and makes things

**evaporate** to turn into vapour

**exchange** a telephone office where telephone calls are connected

**export** to sell a product to another country

**focus** adjust to make a picture or image sharp

**fossil** a print or the remains of an ancient animal or plant, found in rock

**friction** the force which occurs when the surfaces of two objects slide against each other. Friction slows down movement

**fuel** a material that releases energy on burning

**fulcrum** the pivot or point on which a lever is supported

**generate** to produce

**geologist** scientist who studies rocks on and beneath the surface of the Earth

**gravity** the pull on all objects due to the Earth

**grid** the system of linked electricity cables and pylons that allows electricity to be sent over great distances

**horizontal** a level, sideways line, at right-angles to an upright or vertical line

**laser** a device that produces a very bright, narrow beam of light

**lens** a curved piece of glass used in cameras, telescopes or spectacles. The part of the eye which focusses the image

**load** the weight raised or moved by a lever or other machine

**magnetism** a force which occurs in some metals, such as iron. Magnets attract (pull together) or repel (push apart) each other

**mammal** a warm-blooded animal which gives birth to live young and produces milk to feed them

**mesh** to slot together

**muscles** your muscles pull your bones to make them move

**nuclear fuel** a substance which can release energy by a special process. Nuclear fuels do not burn like other fuels

**opaque** something which you cannot see through

**peat** layers of dead plants which have been compressed

**poles** the ends of a magnet where the magnetic force is strongest

**pollution** when substances such as air or water are spoiled or made dirty by people

**prehistoric** before recorded history

**prey** to hunt an animal for food. The hunted animal is also called 'prey'

**pupil** the hole in the centre of the coloured iris in your eye which lets in light

**pylon** tall structure for supporting electricity cables

**refinery** a place where crude oil is made into products such as petrol

**reflect** to bounce back light

**refraction** bending of light

**relay** to broadcast a programme received from another station or source

**renewable energy** energy from a source that will not run out, such as the wind

**reservoir** a large lake where water is stored

**restore** to repair or bring back to the original state

**retina** a light-sensitive layer at the back of the eye

**seam** a layer of coal in rock

**shaft** a metal or wooden bar that passes on movement from one part of an engine to another mechanical part

**spectrum** the seven colours which make up white light

**speed** the distance covered in a certain time measured in m/s or km/h

**static electricity** the effects produced by electric charges which are not moving

**survey** a study of the Earth's surface and rock layers beneath the surface

**temperature** the measurement of 'hotness'

**transfer** to change position, move from one place to another

**translucent** something that lets light through, but is not transparent

**transmitter** a device for sending out radio signals

**transparent** something that lets light through, so that things are clearly seen

**turbine** a wheel with blades, driven by steam (or water, or the wind) which drives machines that generate electricity

**vertical** upright, at right-angles to a horizontal or sideways line

**vibrations** rapid movements forwards and backwards

**water cycle** the movement of water from the sea to the air to the ground and sea, then back to the air

# Index

acceleration 10
Archimedes 17

Baird, John Logie 59
batteries 33
Bell, Alexander Graham 54

cats' eyes 45
central heating 30, 37
coal 6, 24–7, 30, 36
coal mines 23, 26–7
compact discs 51
compass 34
computers 60–1
conduction 40–1
convection 40–1

echoes 48–9
Edison, Thomas 50
electric circuit 5, 33
electric current 33
electric motor 35
electrical signals 50–9
electricity 5, 26, 30–1, 32–9
energy 4–7, 20–1, 22, 24, 33, 37, 40–1
energy transfer 5
evaporation 40

Faraday, Michael 35, 36
fax 53
floating 9
flying 21
forces 8–19
fossil fuels 24
Franklin, Benjamin 32
friction 12–13, 21, 33
fuel 4, 6, 24–31, 37
fulcrum 16–17

gas 25, 28–9, 30–1, 36, 38–9
gears 18–19, 20–1
generating electricity 36–7
geologists 26, 28
Gilbert, William 34
gravity 8–11, 18

hearing 48–9
heat 5, 37, 40–1

laser 51
lenses 46–7
levers 16–17
light 5, 42–3
lightning 5, 33
loads 14–15
lodestone 35
loudspeakers 54–5, 58

machines 12
magnetic metals 34–5
magnetic poles 34–5
magnets 34–5, 36, 50, 55
magnification 46–7
mangonel 17
Marconi, Guglielmo 57
microphones 50, 54, 56
mirrors 44–5, 47
modem 60
Moon 8
Morse, Samuel 52
moving energy 7, 22

Newcomen, Thomas 23
Newton, Sir Isaac 43
newtons 8
nuclear fuels 37
nuclear power 37

Oersted, Hans 35
oil 25, 28–9, 30–1, 36
oil products 30–1
oil refineries 29
oil rigs 28–9

parachutes 21
peat 24–5
pendulum 7
power stations 26, 30, 36–7
pulleys 15

radio 56–7
rainbows 43
reflection 42, 44, 45, 46–7
refraction 45, 46–7
renewable energy 37
reservoir 23

satellites 59
see-saw 16
shadows 42–3
Shaw, Percy 45
sight 46–7
sledges 14, 15
solar power 37
sound 48–51
spectrum 43
speech 48
speed 10–13
static electricity 32–3
steam engine 23
Stephenson, George 23
stored energy 6–7, 24, 25
streamlining 13
Sun 37, 40–1, 42–3
surveying 26, 28

tape recorders 50–1
telegraph 52–3
telephone 54–5, 60
television 58–9
telex 52–3
temperature 41
thermometer 41
transmitters 54, 56–7, 59
trebuchet 17
Trevithick, Richard 23
turbines 23, 36, 37

upthrust 9

video recorders 59
Volta, Alessandro 32
volts 32

water cycle 40
water energy 22–3
water wheel 22–3
Watt, James 23
weight 8–9
wheels 12, 14–15, 18–19
wind energy 20–1
wind farms 37
wind force 11
windmills 20–1